A Walk into April

Poems by

Sam Ragan

St. Andrews Press
Laurinburg, NC

ISBN 0-932662-62-5
Copyright 1986 by Sam Ragan

St. Andrews Press
St. Andrews Presbyterian College
Laurinburg, NC 28352

Printed by Edwards & Broughton, Raleigh, NC

Dedicated To
Marjorie, Nancy, Talmadge, Robin, Eric
And the People of North Carolina

Table of Contents

I

I have seen sunrise,
I have seen moonrise . . .

The Farmer

I have seen sunrise,
I have seen moonrise
From these fields.
You know the old saying:
A farmer works from sun to sun,
A woman's work is never done,
And there's a lot of truth in that.
I have seen her face grow old and tired,
And I ain't what I used to be.
But I love to see things grow.
There have been some good years,
Along with the bad, and there's nothing
Better than looking out over
Green growing fields.
There's something about the land
Which gets inside you and it stays
With you the rest of your life.
This land has been in my family
For over a hundred years.
I sure do hate to lose it.

The Teacher

Some times I say to myself,
What the hell am I doing
Standing up here and looking
Into a room full of blank faces.
Then a light will shine in a pair of eyes,
And before long eager voices
Will be heard, questioning,
Exploring an idea, discovering vistas.
Something has happened.
I don't think I teach them anything,
But I like to think I have helped
Create a climate, and out of that climate
They have started
Learning.

The Election

He didn't get drunk
But once every four years,
On election day.
He would rise early and go
To the polls, drinking hard
All day. By the time
The polls were closed
He would be passed out.
It was his way of expressing an opinion.

The Day Kennedy Was Shot

The shoeshine man at the hatter's
Came out of the door to say,
"The President's been shot."
There was a stricken look on his face.
There was the same look in the newsroom.
All the teletypes were going,
And he crowded up to read
The reports from Dallas.
He went to the telephone and said,
"Let's get out a special, an extra."
The thought kept running through his head,
"We've got to let the people know."
They would want to know everything,
And the next two hours,
Until the extra hit the street,
He was busy with that thought.
There would be time enough later
For lamentations.

The Blues Singer

His eyes would get that faraway look,
A look that went beyond the cotton field,
Beyond the tobacco barn
Where he sat hunched over
Looking into the gathering darkness.
Then would come a low rumble,
And then the words
Deep and clear . . .
   Druther drink muddy water,
   Sleep in a hollow log . . .
That long pause, and the low rumble again:
   Druther drink muddy water,
   Sleep in a hollow log,
   Than stay around here,
   And be treated like a dirty dog.

The Writer

They call it writer's block,
And it is a terrible disease,
Which lasts for days, weeks, months, years.
I have had it several times.
There is nothing worse
Than a blank sheet of paper
Staring at you, and no words coming.
I've had it, but came out of it,
Some times with a word, a nod of a head,
The touch of a hand,
But most of the time God only knows
How or why.
I think I'm cured now.
The cure came when I decided
I didn't have to be perfect.

The Editor

I like to take the raw news
And shape it into a Newspaper,
And on a good day it becomes
Not just a newspaper
But a work of art.
I like to think of it that way.
It is a mirror of my town —
The good, the bad, the reality
Of living and dying.
What people do, what they say,
What they think — it's all there.
I believe that an informed people
Can make the right decisions
About their lives.
That is why we are here,
And we are the record of those lives.

A long time ago a wise old editor said
The function of a newspaper
Is "To print the news and raise hell."
I haven't been able to improve
Upon that definition.

The Governor

I wanted to do good things—
I had it all laid out,
In my mind, on paper . . .
It was all there—
Better schools, hospitals, roads, new industry,
More jobs, better race relations,
A fair shake for everyone,
The good life for everybody.
Some of these things happened . . .
Oh, I had power, but one has to learn
When to use it and when not to use it,
And you learn there are some things
You can do, and some things
You can't do.
And you also learn that government
Has a way of running itself.
Oh, I liked the trappings all right,
There's no denying it,
And it's a great feeling, you know,
When you can drive right up
To the guest box, in your limousine
At a football game.

The General

The old general had been reading
But now he gazed into the distance,
His finger still holding his place on the page.
"I don't like war," he said.
"It never solves anything."
His gaze went back to the distance.
"That may sound strange for me to say," he said.
"I went to three of them."

'We Shall Overcome'

They kept going round and round,
Clapping their hands and chanting,
"Unfair, unfair."
I was angry and hurt —
They had no right to say that
About me and my newspaper.
But later when they gathered
In the park across the street,
Linking arms, swaying, and singing,
"We shall overcome . . . some day,"
I had to applaud.
And after it was over
I went upstairs and sat
Looking out of the window
For a long time.

A Man Of Great Glee

William Faulkner, he said, was a man
Of great glee. Paul told about
That time in Charlottesville
When Faulkner had gone to bed
With his muddy shoes on,
And had pulled a sheet over his face.
He had done it to startle
The distinguished professor
Who was to introduce him that night.

An Evening Of Talk

They were in a room together,
Alike and unalike —
Paul Green, Jonathan Daniels, Gerald Johnson.
A little bourbon and branch,
From time to time, loosened them
And they talked until morning.
They talked and I listened.
It was a splendid evening.

Sugar

It was during the war
And everything was rationed,
But what they talked about the most
Was how hard it was to get sugar.
The man heard the talk over and over,
And he got tired of it.
One day he went into town and bought
All the sugar he was allotted —
Five pounds of it —
And after it had been put into a paper bag
And tied with a string, he went outside,
Waiting until a crowd gathered.
Then he flung the bag of sugar
Against a wall and watched it
Slide down to the ground.
The crowd was outraged,
Said he must be crazy, and somebody
Wanted him arrested, but the policeman
Didn't know what to charge him with,
So he walked away.
"I just wanted to show them," he said.
"That there are things more important than sugar."

The Ultimate Truth

It was Noel Houston who said:
"I love to listen to writers talk.
I have sat for hours listening,
Expecting the ultimate truth
To flower any minute.
But I learned a long time ago
That if that truth doesn't flower
By midnight, I might as well go home,
And start all over again the next day."

My Old Mule Is Dead

They found his body in the pond,
And on the banks there was his jacket
With a note under a rock.
The penciled note told it all:
"My old mule is dead."

. . . only a country man
Can understand that.
The relationship between a man and his mule
Is something special.

On The Street

He was muttering to himself
As they walked along, and she suddenly
Slapped him across the face.
He stood there glowering.
"Now what do you think?" she asked.
"I don't think nothing," he said.
"Oh, yes, you do," she said.
"You think damn."
And she hit him again.

The Witness

She was on the witness stand,
And there was fire in her eyes
As she answered the questions.
She was firm in her denial.
"I'm not a hustler," she said.
"I don't have to hustle —
My sweet little mama —
She's right over there —
She gives me everything
My little heart desires,
From milk in the morning
To pork chops at night."

At The Sawmill

Willie had been showing off
In the green end all morning.
The smell of fresh cut pine
Hung over the mill site
Deep in the woods.
The man at the saw was looking back
As the carriage with the log returned.
He did not hear Willie's scream
Over the scream of the saw,
And he did not see Willie
Until he came running out
Waving the bloody stump, and crying
"Where in the world is my arm?"
But he could look up and see
The arm being carried to the top
Of the sawdust pile, the fingers
Clutching at emptiness
As they moved upward.

The Wedding Dress

That was a long time ago, he said.
I had made no headway with her,
No headway at all.
Then one day she came to me
In the field, and said,
"I'll spend the night with you for five dollars."
It caught me by surprise.
I just stared.
"I'm getting married on Sunday," she said.
"And I need a new dress."

The Sister

She had asked us to go home with her.
It was night time and she needed a ride,
She lived out in the country.
She sat on the back seat and talked.
"I got a sister," she said.
"She twenty year old,
And I hope me die,
She never had a piece."

The Cartoonists

He admired the cartoonists
On the editorial pages,
And he talked about them
As if they were old, admired friends,
Calling their names—
Herblock, Mauldin . . .
"They can say so much," he said.
"One little line
Tells it all."

The Funeral

It was a cold day,
The rain sort of slithered down.
We shivered at the graveside,
And the preacher hurried through the service
Mumbling the words from the prayer book.
It was quickly over, and the undertaker
Motioned to the two men
Standing under the shelter
To come and fill the grave.
We walked away from the tall
Granite stones in the old cemetery,
None of us said anything.
There were only six of us in all.
We had all known this man,
And many others had known him in his time.
But where were they?
Not even his sister came to his funeral.

The Runner

He loved to run,
And he wanted to live forever.
So he ran to be healthy
And to live a long time.
He was the golden boy in the town—
At thirty he was president of the bank,
At thirty-two he owned it,
And he owned a lot of lives as well.
Every day he ran twelve miles
Before breakfast.
Then one morning he came home
From running, took a shower,
Put on his silk bathrobe,
And put a bullet through his head.

The Leaving

It wasn't what she expected at all—
It was no mansion, it was a hovel,
And he wouldn't, or couldn't,
Talk to her.
After eight months she had had enough,
She would go back to Richmond,
Back to her friends, tell them something.
She packed her bag,
And on that May morning
She walked out to the field
Behind the house where he was plowing.
She waited at the end of the row
Until he had pulled the horse to halt.
"I'm leaving you, Will," she said.
He did not say anything.
His eyes said it all,
And he slapped the horse with the line
To start a new furrow.
She did not look back.

Heritage

They came up the river,
And moved out across
The Cape Fear valley and beyond
To become a part of the land
Of the "God-blessed Macs."
They staked out farms and households,
Often with a talisman
Of a name if nothing else
Of the old homeland, their Highlands—
Ballachulish was among them—
The Highland Call was strong,
And they brought with them
Old ways, old beliefs, their music,
A fervent dedication to learning.
But this was a new land,
A new freedom, a new singing
Of the spirit, a new naming of places—
Gum Swamp, Laurel Hill, Old Hundred,
Joe's Creek, Cool Springs, John's—
Families gave their names to places
Where people gathered together
For commerce or communion—
Laurinburg, Gibson, Elmore, and others,
A blending of the old and the new,
Coming together under the name
Of their ancient Celtic homeland—Scotland.
It was a land of the McCalls, McLaurins,
And other Macs, a people close to the land,
And some stayed and some moved away,
But always returning in memory,
In renewal of time and ties,
And a day of remembering.

II

. . . the innocence of morning

Morning Collection

I was awake early
To the innocence of morning,
Collecting that innocence,
The colors and sounds
And storing them away
For noon time, afternoons and nights.

Nathaniel Macon

It's time to move on, he said,
When you can hear your neighbor's dog bark.
Old Nathaniel Macon lived
Far out in the country,
And he didn't stay in Washington
Any more than he had to —
He was Jefferson's friend,
And there were letters between them.
He had power in Washington
As Speaker of the House,
But Warren was his home,
And it was where he returned.
He didn't want any funeral when he died,
And no monument on his grave.
But, he said, if anyone should pass this way
And think kindly of me,
Let them toss a stone
On my resting place.

That was long ago, and there's
A big pile of rocks in Warren County.

Homecoming

They all come back
To Old Bethesda,
And on this autumn afternoon
Of sunshine and homecoming
The man from California is saying:
My grandfather was born here.
He told me stories, over and over,
Until I got to know this place
Better than I knew my own.
I had to come and see.

Return To April

All the way through this April afternoon,
Driving through Orange County
And on to Raleigh, I think
With each returning spring
I, too, return,
Not so much to place or time
But to that sense of wonder.
I do not ask how long it will last,
It is enough to climb that far hill
And see how even now the new green of trees
Are speckled against the sky
Seven miles away.

Measurements

Into the places where only the rocks rear
And the wind blows silently,
Fitfully soft, and only the sun
Has such a hard eye.
No trees —
Only the bush that snares
The roaming weed.
Such is the mind that counts the coin
And measures happiness
By the little black ink entry
In the ledger book.

The Leaves Do Not Cry

A cold wind came up
And when the rain had gone
The moon's light caught the color
Of wet leaves.
I had walked through them when they were dry,
But now they do not cry
When I walk upon them.

Home Is Where You Hang Your Childhood

Someone said it a long time ago:
Home is where you hang your childhood.
It's a place where memories fused
Into other memories,
And not a place for going back.
Even on sun-spattered days
Everything is smaller.

Black And White

The big black dog comes loping
Across the snow.
He is curious about the strangeness
Of a familiar place,
And he wavers in his tracks,
His head swinging from side to side.
The snow comes down.
The dog is suddenly gone.
His tracks fill up.
The world is white again.

The Road That Leads Away

That summer with the timeless turn,
All the way back from Waccamaw
Where the dance ended
When a fight broke out, and someone
Was pushed into the lake,
They were all laughing.
Later when walking down the hall
He heard the old man snoring
Next door to the girl who was crying
And he had stopped, almost knocking,
But he went on.
The next morning the girl was gone,
And the old man sat rocking on the porch,
His eyes looking beyond the courthouse,
Beyond the street turn
That leads from town.

Done With Apple-Picking

I put down the book
And see the September moon
Rising slightly red
Beyond the stilled pines.
I have been reading the poet
Who talked of apple-picking,
And mending walls, the bending of birches,
Of pasture springs and other things . . .

But I am done with apple-picking now.

The moon has gone higher.
And far off in the night,
In the valley of Aberdeen
A dog is barking.

A Happening

The college had asked me
To come and conduct a happening,
And I asked you
(You were ten at the time)
What is a happening?
And you said,
"A happening is throwing ice cream
     on a naked lady."

Nancy

You talked about bluebirds
When you were three—
And the bright bluebird
Winging into the sunlight
Always seems a part of you.
There was that song,
"Nancy With the Laughing Face,"
Which brightened dark days of long ago,
And other sights and sounds
Flood the memories
Of someone very special.
It has been a wonderful journey,
And it's the journey that counts,
Not the getting there.
Here at home the dogwood is in bloom,
And across the miles I am proud
That others share my pride in you—
The very special you.

Randall Jarrell

The honored poet
Was the center of attention
At the dinner.
We hurried ahead to find a seat
In the fast-filling hall
Where the tributes were to be paid.
But a look backward stands in our memory
More than what was said.
Randall Jarrell and his Mary
Were holding hands as they walked
Into the twilight.

A Christmas Night

It was a cold night
And there was ice on the road,
Our car started to slide
As it moved up the small hill,
And the headlights caught the old man
In a thin jacket
Pushing a cart filled with sticks.
There were some bundles and a package
Piled on top, and the old man
Grinned and waved at us
As he pushed the cart
Into the yard of the little house
Where a single light shone.
The tires gripped the road
And we drove on into the darkness,
But suddenly it was warm.

John Patrick's Walnut Trees

The founder of the town had planted them—
Five black walnut trees had survived
More than one hundred years.
One had died at the century mark,
But the others still had their ungainly beauty,
The bare stark branches against the sky
Had a special appeal, and the avenue
Along which they stood was enhanced
By their presence.
But the town fathers knew they were old
And perhaps would soon die,
So they were ordered cut down.
He resisted them for more than a year,
But finally gave in after promises were made
That new red maples would take their place,
And their timber would be saved
For historic artifacts. But he stayed away
The morning they came down. It was too much to watch.
And then, a neighbor came with a pot
In which a seedling grew — he had saved
Some of the walnuts and they had sprouted.
Now that seedling is more than two feet tall,
It will be nursed to manhood,
And a link to John Patrick.

A Ring For Each Year

A tree grows slowly—
They say a ring for each year.
But there are other measurements
For other things and people—
How well we serve others
Is a long honored yardstick.
In the cycles and recycling
Of time started long ago,
Or perhaps only yesterday,
We are a part of all we have met.
In old Alamance through which the Haw
Flows seaward, where October
Is a cherished month,
We can measure time by things we keep
And use again over and over,
With the old serving the new,
Just as this house
Is put again to use
As an honored place
Serving others.

History From A Hilltop

From the hilltop we could see
For miles across the trees,
And at night the highway
Was a ribbon of lights
Running to the city's sky glow.
But we were looking backward
Where there were no lights, only a surging
From the sea and down the valleys,
The knottings of people in common cause,
In communion and conflict,
Coming and going, shaping and reshaping
A place, a time, a people.

How do we tell their story?
That was the question before us—
Telling the story through the camera's eye—
And each of us had a different answer.
Episodes out of a past that shaped
A present and a future.
Each saw an event, an incident, as a turning point,
A shaper of other events.
The list was long:
The coming of the railroad,
A constitutional convention,
Tobacco, cotton mills,
Violence in Gastonia,
Violence in Marion . . .
All bits and pieces from the past,
The fits and starts of four hundred years,
Documents and drama dropped down
In uneven segments of time—
But never a flow,
Never a flow of lights.

III

There are still travelers

Face Sleeping

I was awake early,
But before I arose
I watched your face sleeping.
I cannot remember when your face
Has not been there.
I drink coffee and watch
The sun come up.
I feel a warm glow.

Let Us Walk Into April

It was a pear tree in bloom
That lit up your eyes.
You came at blossom time—
Dogwoods and lilacs,
The camellia and azalea,
And the glow of the redbud tree—
Thousands of wildflowers run before your feet,
And a faint green hovers in the woods.
Here we are just before the coming of April,
When the whole world is new
And each day is a beginning,
A time of sunlight and splendor—
Come, let us walk into April.

The Tally Of Our Days

We have taken the measurements
Of each greening Spring,
Recorded the calendar turns,
And marked each season
With its own talisman.
Here on the eve of April
The flowers have their messages
To add to their light-footed
Tally of our days
In this journey.
You have come into this special time
And given it a meaning all its own.
I count the seasons, past and future,
Let us keep on with the markings.

Voices

In all these rains tonight,
In all these wind-blown rains
That drench the trees—
And I can see by lightning light
Such silhouettes of darkness
That stand as sentinels to mark
Each troubled lost step—
Hear, Hear among the rumble
Of close by thunder,
Voices coming closer,
Closer.

For Remembering

I stand at the window and watch
Summer explode across the lawn.
A dog lopes through the meadow,
A bird wings to the woods,
And nothing else moves
On this afternoon
Of summer sun and summer heat.
I turn away and mark it down
For remembering
When these same fields
Are filled with snow.

The Cardinal

That flash of color, bright red,
In the green of the pines
Was a cardinal pursuing
Something we could not see;
But in the fading sunlight
He was quickly come and quickly gone,
Only his cry from the far woods
Coming back to me
In the settling darkness
Of this May night.

The Storm

The storm came up quickly,
Bringing the darkness early.
The rolling thunder came closer and closer,
Lightning crackled, its fingers
Jabbing their way
Across the sky.
The wind brought the rain,
And we ran for the open doorway,
Pushing it shut against the wind.
At the window we watched
The twisting and turning trees,
The lightning coming to earth
And sending us reeling backward.
But we had to watch, and soon
We could see through the rain,
And the thunder had gone
Muttering to the east,
Just as other furies
In other times
Had come and gone.